*N.B. **The diagrams heading the several pages are designed to show how the principles and l***

also to indicate the analysis of the letters. First principle.   52°   *Oblique Straight l*

marks parallel to each other. Write the principles and letters, excepting **r** and **s**, within the wide spaces as in

MW01046484

All the curves in this book, constituting letters or parts of letters and commencing on the base line, are single and of the same length.

Right Curve. Left Curve.

Second Principle—Right Curve. 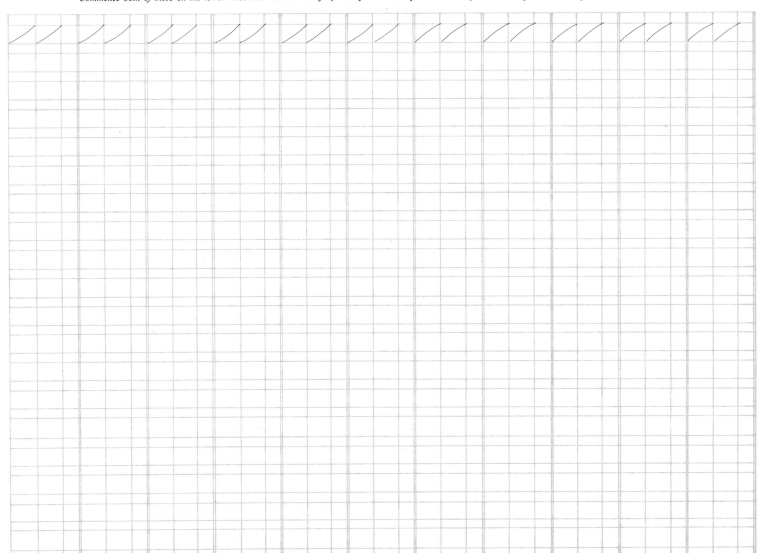 *Third Principle—Left Curve.*

Commence both of these on the lower ruled line. Observe carefully their forms and adjust them closely to the ruling as in the diagram. Count 1, 2, 1, 2, etc.

In the diagrams following study the analysis of the letters.

The figures in the **diagrams** indicate the **Principles.**

The Second Principle (⟋) is prefixed to the First (╱)

Make letters without shade. Count 1, 2, 1, dot.

joining it at the top and then affixed to the same by a

short connecting curve at the base. This curve we call the lower turn; it occupies about one-sixth of a space. See second page of our cover for full explanation.

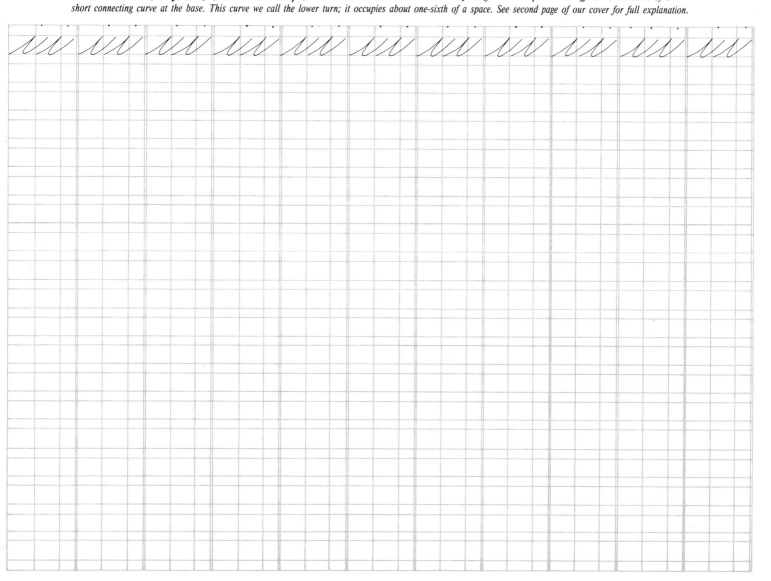

4

Study the Diagrams and learn how to adjust the letters to the ruling.

Width of **u** one space. Second Principle unites 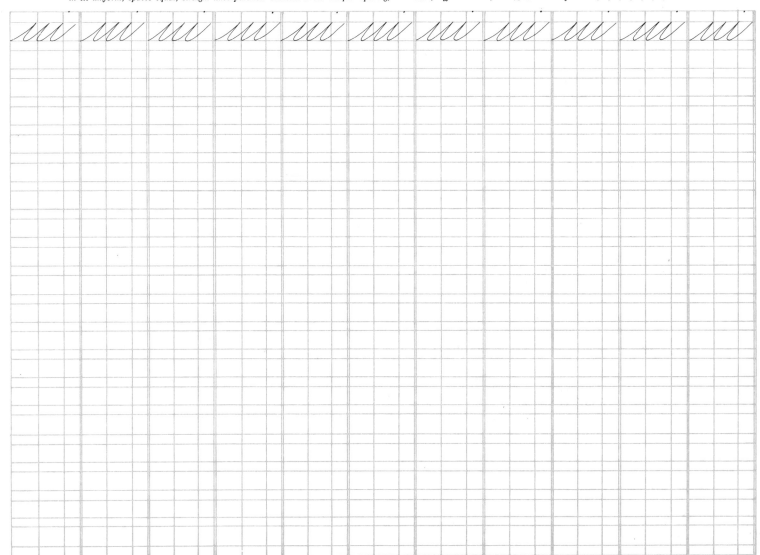 with first at top as in **i**, **w**, and **a**. Make the turns in **ui** uniform, spaces equal, straight lines parallel. Caution: avoid unequal spacing, thus *uu*; different slant, thus *uu*. Count for **ui** 1, 2, 3, 4, 1, 2, 1, dot.

Analysis of w.

Write with a careful movement.
Width of w one space and a half. Turns in iw alike.

Count for iw 1, 2, 1, 2, 3, 4, 5, dot 1, dot.
Straight lines parallel and equally distant.

Finish the w with a small dot and the Second Principle in horizontal position. Avoid unlike turns, thus ⱳⱳⱳ; a loop in w instead of a dot, thus ⱳⱳ.

*Analysis of **n**.*

Width of **n** one space. Third Principle (/) unites
upper turn. It again unites angularly with the same at

the First (/) at top by a short curve called the
base. The upper turn occupies same space as lower turn.

*Make straight lines in **ni** parallel and equally spaced, turns uniformly alike. The accuracy of this copy may be tested by inverting it. Count for **ni** 1, 2, 3, 4, 1, 2, 1 dot.*

*Analysis of **m**.*

Width two spaces. Upper turns same as in **n**. Third Principle [diagram] unites with first at base. Curve lines same in length. Avoid unlike turns, slope and spacing. The aim, in this course of practice, should be to make each successive word and line bear distinctly the stamp of improvement. Count 1, 2, 3, 4, 5, 6, 1.

8

Analysis of x.

Think and write.
Make the turns exactly alike both at top and base,
Cross upward with a straight line through middle of First Principle on same slant with the curve lines. See that the upper and lower turns are short and alike.

Count 1, 2, 1, Cross.
and as short as possible with continuous motion.

Analysis of *v*.

Width from turn to dot half a space. 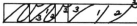 Upper and lower turns alike.

Dot and finish same as in **w**. Be careful not to make the opening too wide at the top, thus ∿ ; the sides unequal in height, thus ⋏ . Count 1, 2, 3, dot 1.

Analysis of o.

Width one-third of the length. Opposite sides equally 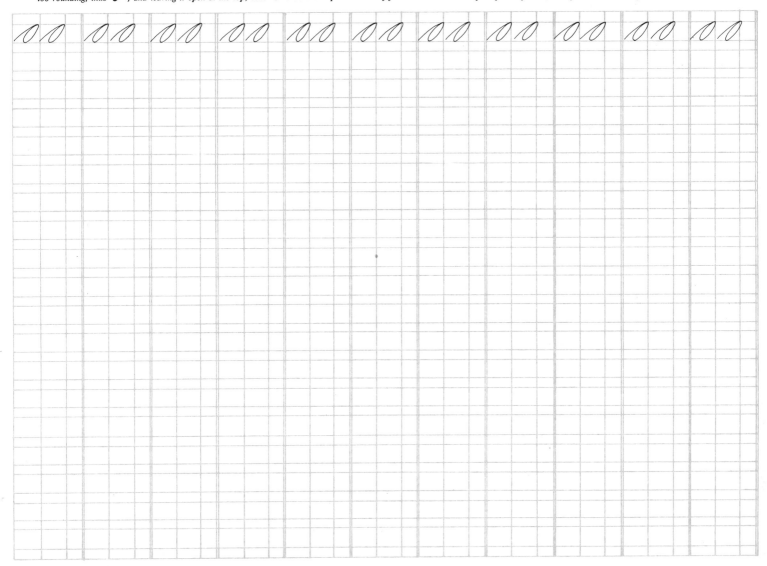 *curved and closed at the top. Caution: avoid making the letter too rounding, thus σ ; and leaving it open at the top, thus σ . Correct representation of forms involves correct perception of them; therefore, think when you write. Count 1, 2, 3.*

*Analysis of **a**.*

Width of a one space. Slant the oval same as Second 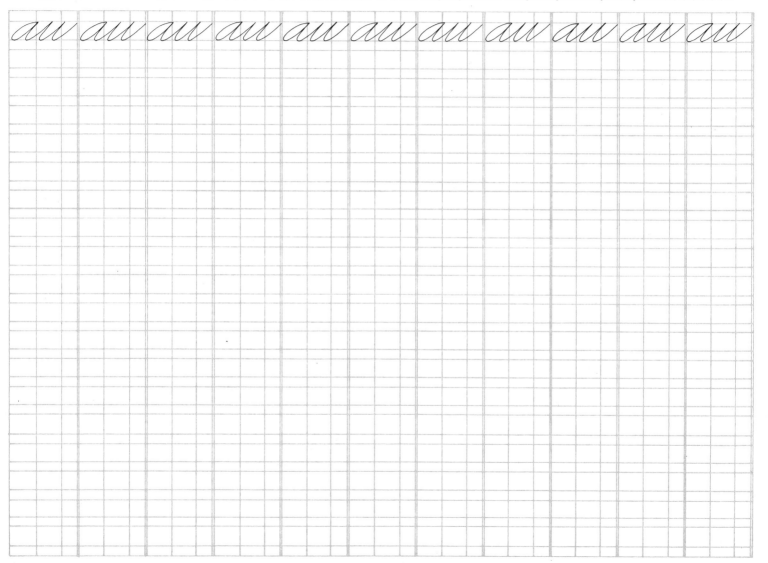 Principle in **w**. Curve the left side fuller than the right.
*Right curve in **au** united with straight line at top throughout. In straight lines preserve uniformity of slant and spacing, and avoid leaving the **a** open at the top. Count for **au** 2, 1, 2, 1, 2, 3, 4, 1.*

12

Analysis of *e*.

Width one-third of space. 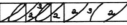 Loop two thirds of length.

Left curve same as in **o** and **c**. Turn short as possible at top and base without stopping. Avoid too full a curve on the left, which makes too wide a loop, thus *ℓ* . Count 1, 2, 1.

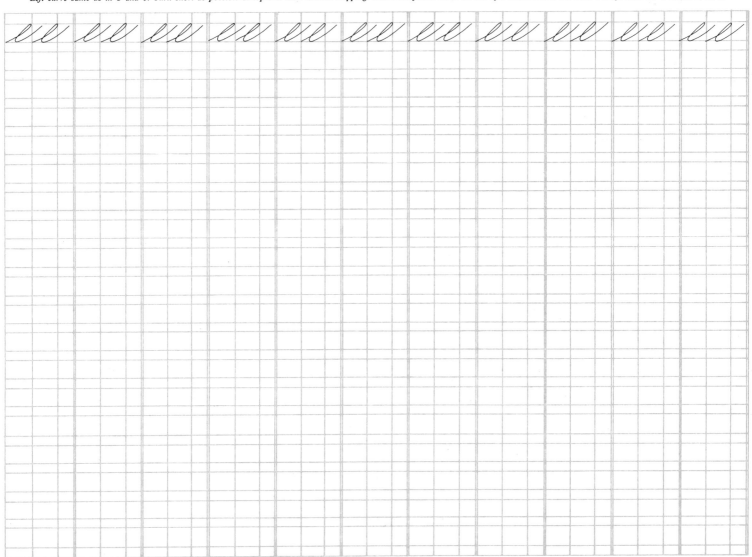

*Analysis of **c**.*

Width half a space. Oval [diagram] turn at top occupies one-third of space from upper line. Loop two-thirds the height same as **e**. Turns above and below short. Caution: avoid making the top too large, thus ℮ . Count 1, 2, 3, 4, 1.

Analysis of r.

Width half a space. Carry Second Principle one-fourth 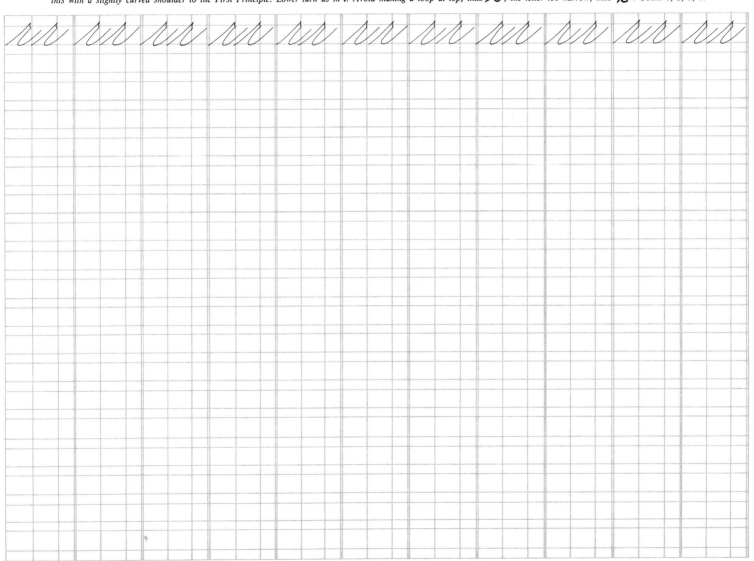 of a space above upper line. Make a small dot, and join this with a slightly curved shoulder to the First Principle. Lower turn as in **i**. Avoid making a loop at top, thus ✗ ; the letter too narrow, thus ✗ . Count 1, 2, 3, 1.

Analysis of s.

Width half a space.
one-fourth of a space above upper line. Downward line
terminates in a dot one-fourth of a space above lower line. Caution: avoid loop at top, thus *ᶫ* . Second Principle should not lean too far to the right, thus *ᶦ* . Count 1, 2, 3, dot 1.

Second Principle
diverges from top of Second Principle, and, after the turn,

*Write words without lifting the pen. Observe the inclination of the left side of **a**,*
*the height of **r** and its peculiar shoulder. Pupils should form the habit of criticising their own writing. Count for air 2, 1, 2, 1, 2, 1, 2, 3, 1, dot.*

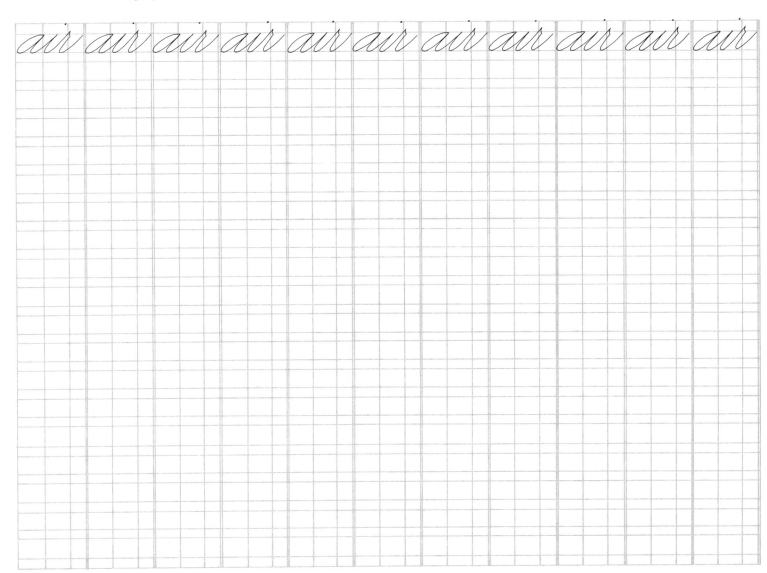

Pass with a single curve line directly under
the dot in the **s**, and so connect it with the **e** as in the copy, not thus *see* . Make all the letters here, as elsewhere, very light. Count 1, 2, 3, dot 1, 2, 1, 2, 1.

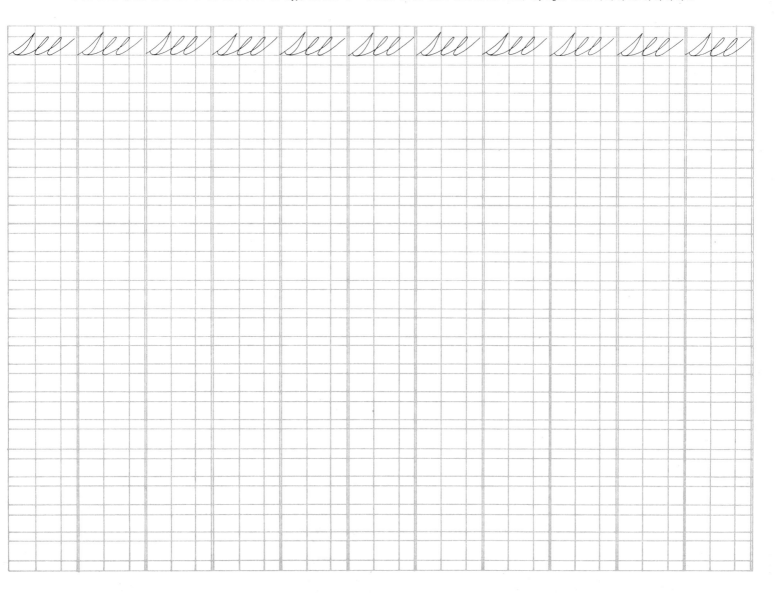

18

Study carefully every part of every letter—every Principle engaged in its production. Count 1, 2, 3, 4, 1, 2, 1.

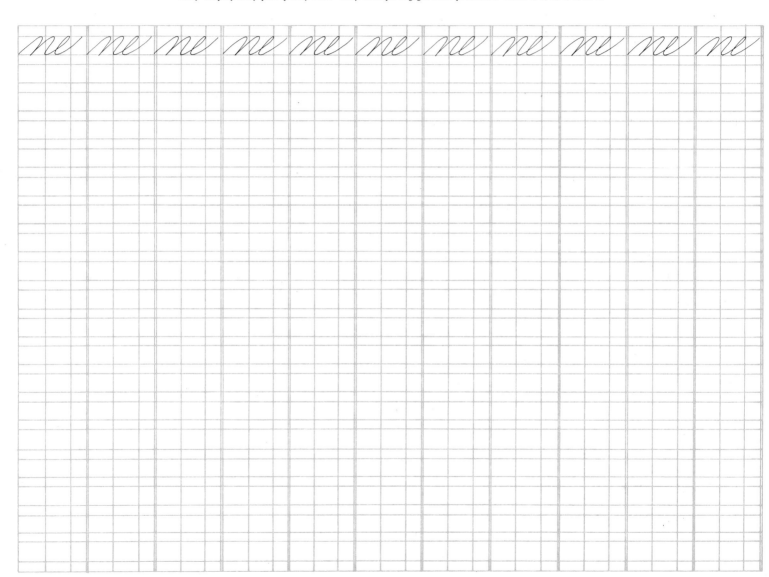

Make top of c small and Third Principle slightly curved. The dot of i should be small and neatly made. Secure correctness of form, height, slant and spacing. Count 1, 2, 1, 2, 3, 4, 1, 2, 1.

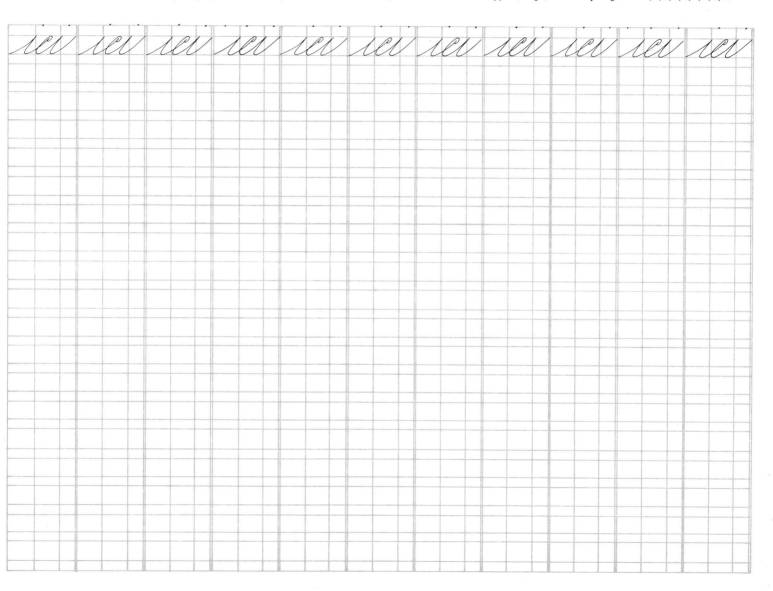

*Make the turns uniform in **x** and **v**,*
*cross **x** with an upward movement. Make **v** one-half space. Study carefully here, as elsewhere, every part of every letter. Count for **x** 1, 2, 1, cross; for **v** 1, 2, 3, dot 1.*

Observe how the **o** and **w** are connected by Second Principle
in horizontal position. Close **o** at top. Straight lines and dot in **w** should always touch upper line, not thus 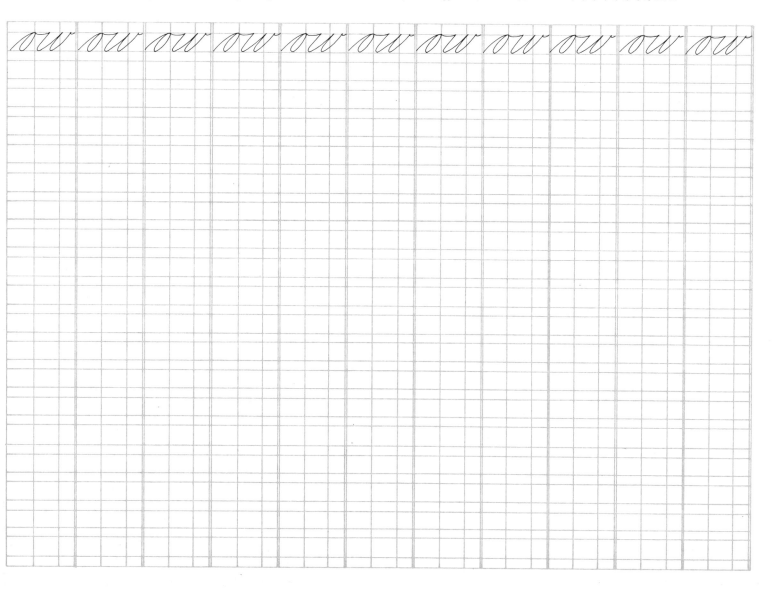 . Count 1, 2, 3, 1, 2, 3, 4, 5, dot 1.

*See that the curved lines in **u** are parallel and of the same length. Observe the height and width of the **s**, and the form and position of the dot. Count 1, 2, 3, 4, 1, 2, 3, dot 1.*

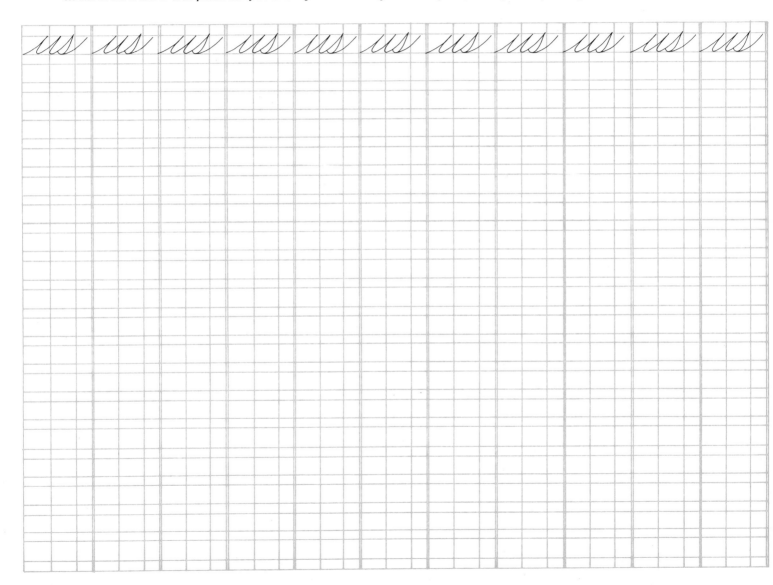

Observe particularly how and where the curve and straight lines unite;
also the equal spaces between straight lines when connected by single curves. Write this copy so that it will bear the test of inversion. Count 1, 2, 3, 4, 1, 2, 1 dot.

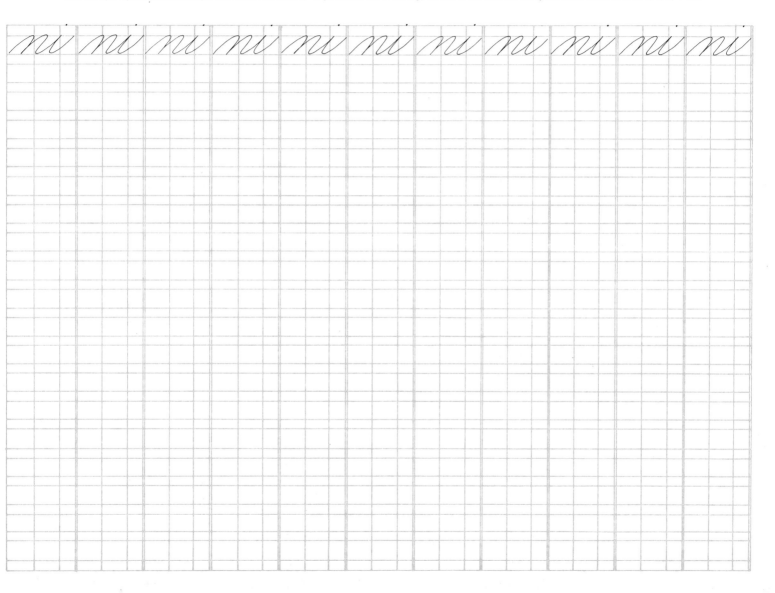

Here note especially the turns, slant and spacing. Make this page the best in the book. The last effort should always show decided improvement on all the former.